To all the little ballerinas who work hard everyday.
Shine bright like the stars you are!

ISBN: 978-1-7345572-0-6

First Edition

Curly & Confident Publishing
860 Johnson Ferry Road
Ste 140-370
Atlanta GA 30342

A division of Beautiful Curly Me LLC
https://www.beautifulcurlyme.com

CURLY + CONFIDENT publishing

IMARA BALLERINA
The Big Dance

By Zoe Oli

Illustrated by Adesewa Adekoya

CURLY + CONFIDENT publishing

Imara is excited!
Today is a big day.

Her first ballet recital
was finally here!

She's been working hard all year
and can't wait
to show everyone all she's learned

After lunch,
Mom brings out
her costume

It has purple sequins that sparkle,

and a fluffy tutu that blooms

"It's so pretty!", Imara said
as she smiled and thanked her mom

But as she opened the box
with her ballet tights and shoes,
something seemed wrong.

"They're brown?!
Other dancers wear pink,

I need to look the same!"
Imara said with a frown.

"But why?" Mom asked,

“These tights and shoes are the perfect blend for your pretty cocoa skin.

Vibrant as the morning sun,
rich like the deep brown soil,

your skin is beautiful
and more than anything
you belong."

"But, won't I look different?
Won't I look strange?"
Imara wondered out loud

Her Mom replied,
“Being different is a superpower,
and being you should make you proud!

"Mom's right!", Imara realized
and she just couldn't wait
to be on stage that night.

She put on her costume
and twirled about,
feeling like a prima ballerina
without a doubt.

As the curtains rose,
Imara smiled brightly,
remembering her mother's words;

It was time to shine
and be the star
she always knew she was.

She flew through the air
in her *grand jetes,*

and performed her *pirouettes* gracefully on stage.

Words used in the book

Pirouettes - **pir·ou·ette - /ˌpir'wet/**

When a dancer spins around fast on one foot

Grand Jetes - **grand je·té - /gräN ZHe'tā/**

A high leap with your toes pointed

MEET THE AUTHOR

Zoe Oli is the 10 year old CEO of Beautiful Curly Me - an Atlanta-based Toy and media company on a mission to instill and inspire confidence in young girls. She founded her company at age 7 with her Mom's help after overcoming challenges with self-esteem. Zoe is the author of 2 other children's books: "Beautiful Curly Me" and "Say it, Show it: A Guided Gratitude & Kindness Journal for Kids".

Zoe has been featured on various media outlets including Forbes, Good Morning America, People, The Kelly Clarkson Show, and Black Enterprise and she was recently named a Time and Nickelodeon Kid of The Year Finalist.

In line with her mission to raise the next generation of curly and confident girls, for every doll purchased on beautifulcurlyme.com, one is donated to a young girl in need.

An active 6th grader who loves reading, art, music, and all things STEM, Zoe also enjoys tennis, traveling, and giving back to the community.

More from Zoe!

I hope you enjoyed this book! Like Imara, keep your confidence shining with more empowering products and books written by me.

Beautiful Brown Ballet - 64 piece puzzle
Fun puzzle celebrating Imara and her 2 friends on the big stage!

Beautiful Curly Me is a book for curly girls to celebrate all the things that make them special.

Say it Show it Gratitude & Kindness Journal
Make gratitude and kindness a daily habit with this 90-day journal filled with prompts and challenges.

Curly + Confident Clubhouse STEAM 100-piece puzzle
Join Imara and her friends in the clubhouse where everyone gets to explore their passions.

Girls Affirmation Puzzle
Handcrafted wooden puzzle with powerful words you can say to yourself everyday.

Find these and many more at **beautifulcurlyme.com**